QUIT GAMBLING QUIT RELAPSING

Straightforward & Practical Lessons To Change The Perspective & Habits Of Persons With A Gambling Disorder

Quit Gambling Quit Relapsing. Straightforward & Practical Lessons To Change The Perspective & Habits Of Persons With A Gambling Disorder.

GAMBLING IS A BUSINESS. IT PROFITS ITS OWNER NOT THE CUSTOMER.

Gambling is a billion-dollar industry built on the tears of losers. **It is NOT designed to help you achieve financial security.** It is not designed to help you at all. It is a business that sells very expensive entertainment.

The games are designed to benefit the Owners. **Every time you play, THEY win.** Every cent you wager improves their lives. Your money goes into their pockets so that they can live luxuriously while you suffer, beg and borrow.

Your money allows them to buy mansions, luxury cars and designer clothes. They use your savings to vacation in exotic locations and to drape themselves in diamonds, while you figure out how to stretch a dollar until your next pay day.

You depend on luck, hope and wishes while they operate on certainty. **As long as you keep showing up, they can be certain that their bills will be paid.**

You spend hours every day playing their games and competing with the other gamblers for CRUMBS. Meanwhile, the Owners are out living full lives. They are eating the juicy steak and drinking the champagne that you paid for.

Every business exists to MAKE / EARN money. They either sell you a product or provide a service. The price they charge the customer covers production costs, employee wages and includes a profit for the Owners.

The Gambling Industry, like every other business, exists to earn money, not to give it away. The Owners of casinos and gaming stations are selling you entertainment in order to make their profit. They're selling an experience ... a good time. There is no fixed cost attached. You can pay as much as you want, whenever you want.

This entertainment that they're selling, provides a small opportunity for you to win back some of the money you spent. You convinced yourself that you could come out on top and take an endless supply of money from them. You forgot your place as a Customer who is actually purchasing the entertainment that they're selling.

The house is designed to win. The odds are rigged in their favor. The Gambling Industry continues to exist because business is good. They are making BILLIONS of dollars in profits because there are more people losing than there are winning.

Game designers are loyal to the companies that hire them. They go to work every day and program games with YOU in mind. Their goal is to keep you invested in the game. They don't want to take all of your money at once. **They program the games to feed you crumbs, so that you continue to play.** You hold on to these small wins without realizing that you are losing more in the long run.

Games are programmed to have frequent near-misses, where you fall just a little bit short of a jackpot. These near-misses toy with your brain. Game designers know that near-misses are highly motivating and increase your commitment to the game. They know that it is hard for you to walk away when you believe that the win will come on the next round.

Games are often designed where you can make multiple types of wagers at the same time. Some betting options may be simple but will have a lower payout, while some are riskier and offer greater rewards. Game designers know that the average person is risk averse and will spread out their money to cover safer options as well as those which have higher payouts.

The result is that a player can win on some lines while losing on others. The winnings will often be less than the original wager. When you win, you still don't come out ahead. These are losses disguised as wins. The lights and sounds of victory come on to make you feel good, but in the grand scope of things, you have lost.

Casinos pump oxygen into their rooms to keep you energetic and awake. They keep the air conditioning chilly to give the same effect. Alcohol is served freely because it eases tension and loosens inhibitions. Music is cranked up loudly so that you never get weary. It competes with the voice in your head, making it difficult for your conscience to be heard.

The electronic gaming machines use sounds that vary in length and loudness to increase excitement and encourage you to play faster. They have no clocks present in the casino for you to glance at because they want you to be fully involved in the game for hours.

The casinos are beautiful and lavish because they are making a profit. **If gambling was benefiting the players, then business would be bad for the Owners and they would close down.**

YOU WILL
NEVER
BE ABLE
TO
CONTROL
YOUR
GAMBLING.

The Diagnostic and Statistical Manual of Mental Disorders, Fifth Edition (DSM-5) is published by the American Psychiatric Association and is the handbook used by health care professionals around the world as the authoritative guide to the diagnosis of mental disorders.

To meet the criteria for a Gambling Disorder diagnosis, an individual has to have at least four of the problems identified below, within a 12-month period, in addition to persistent and recurrent gambling behavior that leads to clinically significant impairment or distress.

The gambler:

*Needs to gamble with increasing amounts of money in order to achieve the desired excitement.

*Is restless or irritable when attempting to cut down or stop gambling.

*Has made repeated unsuccessful efforts to control, cut back or stop gambling.

*Is often preoccupied with gambling, mentally reliving past gambling experiences, planning their next venture or thinking of ways to get money with which to gamble.

*Often gambles when feeling distressed (e.g., helpless, guilty, anxious, depressed).

*After losing money gambling, often returns another day to get even ("chasing" one's losses).

*Lies to conceal the extent of involvement with gambling.

*Has jeopardized or lost a significant relationship, job or educational / career opportunity because of gambling.

*Relies on others to provide money to relieve desperate financial situations caused by gambling.

Mild: 4–5 criteria met.
Moderate: 6–7 criteria met.
Severe: 8–9 criteria met.

Your family and friends will be the first to notice your behavior and say that you have a gambling problem but **an official diagnosis can ONLY come from a qualified practitioner**, who uses the DSM-5 as their guide. No online quiz or support group can issue a diagnosis. Even if all the boxes check off, you must seek the expertise of a qualified practitioner in order to be diagnosed.

You've invested in your game for years, believing that if you play enough, the Big Win will come. You might even believe that you are owed a Big Win.

When you experience a huge loss, you tell yourself that you're done but return to the game shortly afterwards. You exist in a state of conflict where you want to quit but also want to continue playing. You believe that you can control your gambling or at least hope that it is possible to do so.

When the ship is sinking it is wise to get off. Jump into the life raft and sail away. You don't stay aboard a sinking vessel and hope that it stays afloat. You do what is necessary to preserve your life and you do it quickly.

Refer to the DSM-5 guideline for the diagnosis of a Gambling Disorder. If it describes you, then it's clear you have a problem. You will never be able to balance or manage your gambling. It will ALWAYS spiral out of control and bring devastation to your life.

You are not like everyone else.
You belong to the 1% of the population who has a gambling disorder.

The average person can play for 10 minutes and walk away but you CANNOT. You are accustomed to playing for hours, draining your savings and wagering your last dollar.

Your mindset is different. You are more susceptible to greed. When it comes to gambling, you will always crave bigger risks, bigger thrills and bigger wins. **No win will ever be enough to satisfy you. Your mind will always be convinced that you can go back and get more.**

Even if you were to win millions in the lottery and be set for life, you would continue to play. You would do it to test your luck and justify it because you know that you have money to fall back on.

When attempting to control your gambling, you might set a budget and a specific amount of time to play. The minute you start to lose, your brain will go into panic mode. You will invest more and more money to recoup your losses and will stay in the game for as long as it takes for you to lose everything.

Your brain only knows to walk away when you have nothing left to wager. Still, it cannot fully accept defeat. You will get money to play by any means, even if you have to borrow, lie or steal. Logic and common sense take a back seat to your desire for getting even. You will invest as much money as you have available, to ensure that you get a win.

You will try to recoup your losses and trap yourself in this endless cycle of torment. You will NEVER be able to control your gambling. The game will always have the upper hand because it is designed to be like that.

DO YOU GENUINELY WANT TO STOP OR DO YOU JUST HATE LOSING?

The desire to quit always comes after a terrible loss. When you're up and experiencing a streak of good luck, you never want to walk away and put the bets behind you. This begs the question: Do you genuinely want to stop gambling or do you just hate losing?

Do you pledge to quit because in that moment of losing your money, you realize that gambling has cost you too much?

Do you feel guilty in that moment but bounce right back to the game after the guilt has subsided?

Does quitting only cross your mind when you think about your losses or is it something that you have a strong desire to do even when you win?

For most gamblers, quitting becomes an emotional response, like the tantrum thrown by a child who doesn't get their way.

Quitting that is tied to a loss will not last because it is not grounded in logic. As soon as the negative emotions wear off, the urge to gamble will pop up and you will give in.

Think about the reasons why you want to quit. Search yourself and figure out if quitting is really what YOU want.

No outside pressure or ultimatum from loved ones has the power to truly stop you. No program will be effective until you make that choice to stop for good because you want to stop, for your own good.

Always remember that you have free will.
You have the choice to quit or to continue gambling. If your family pressures you to stop and you don't, then they can leave. You can always get a new spouse and have more children. You can always gain new friends and even get new jobs. Let's be real here. You will always have access to money and can always find a way to play.

But is the game really worth losing everything that you currently have? Is it worth having to lie, steal or borrow money and incur debts that you have to struggle to repay? Is the game worth all the pain?

You are not obligated to quit gambling.
It is a choice that you have to make and genuinely want, especially when you're on your good days and have money in your hand.

YOU
ARE
NOT
A
VICTIM.

You are not a victim.
Nobody forces you spend hours gambling away all of your money. You make the conscious decision to do that.

Gambling is not something that just happens to you. It is not a disease like cancer which can still progress in spite of treatment and lead to death.

Your problems are created because of your unwillingness to say no to the game. At some point you have to face these truths and hold yourself accountable for your actions.

Casinos and gambling sites are businesses and they have the right to advertise. They have a right to market their services and to seek out new customers just like every other business. They are not obligated to care about you and they do not owe anything to your recovery.

Your recovery is YOUR business.
Focus on yourself and your healing and allow other people to do what benefits them.

Accountability starts with “I”.
The gambler often says, “Gambling is ruining my life.” Accountability says, “I am ruining my life by choosing to gamble.”

Let go of the victim mentality.
You made deliberate choices and those choices have consequences. Make better choices and watch your life change for the better.

You are so much more powerful than you give yourself credit for. Right now you’re in a dark hole, feeling like you’re being buried in debt because of this constant urge to waste your money. But you are a competent and powerful human being who possesses the ability to change something that is very important. You have the power to change your thoughts. **Change the way you think and you WILL change your life.**

You are the only one capable of fixing your circumstances. You have the ability to heal all of the things that are broken but it will not happen by wishing, hoping and feeling sorry for yourself. There has to be a change in behavior, which can only occur when you purposely create a shift in your mindset.

Stop identifying as an addict.
There is no power in this label. It is a negative term that has no positive value. It only encourages people to scorn and humiliate the ones who carry the label.

Walk around introducing yourself as a compulsive gambler or as a gambling addict and watch how fast opportunities are taken away from you. People will immediately think of you as unreliable and untrustworthy. Instead of being treated with compassion, you will be stripped of your dignity and treated as a degenerate.

There are gamblers who hide behind the word addiction as a way to avoid accountability and to make it seem like there is no choice involved. The word is used as a crutch to stay in the game, to stay weak and to manipulate others into being sympathetic. But loved ones eventually grow tired of giving passes. They will stop caring about how hard quitting is for you. It will be easier for them to walk away and save themselves from your mess.

You can admit that you have a problem and receive help without branding yourself for life, and carrying the stigma of the “addiction” label.

FOCUS
ON
WHAT
YOU
WANT
MORE
OF.

Are you currently working towards a healthy, gamble free life? Or are you thinking of yourself as an addict and running from the gambling demon?

Whatever you focus on will grow.
If you think about the game all the time, or wonder how the machines are playing, then your urge to gamble will grow. You will never be free if you keep thinking about your losses and hoping that one last bet could fix your problems.

If your focus is on your "sickness" then you are not actively making room for wellness. You will remain in bondage if you speak constantly about your struggles to quit and hold on to the false belief that quitting is hard.

To be well and free you have to think, speak and act in ways that produce wellness and freedom.

Instead of "trying to quit", focus on the healthier things that you can do instead of gambling. Stop running from the bad and hoping that it will leave you alone.

Walk towards what is healthy and good.

People will say hurtful things to you and about you, but your perception of yourself is what matters above everything else. If you consider yourself a loser, a failure and a reject, then this is who you will ultimately become. This is the essence of the Self-Fulfilling Prophecy, as taught in Psychology. **The way you think about yourself, good or bad, is who you will eventually be.**

If you believe that you are an addict who cannot do anything right, then Life will give you more opportunities to prove this to be true. If you believe that you are powerless and will never be free from throwing away your money behind a bet, then you will remain in bondage.

Freedom from a gambling disorder is possible.
You can be free to the point where the game doesn't cross your mind. Free from the itch and urge to play. You can be free to find pleasure in doing regular things without wagering and depending on luck.

Ultimately, your success and freedom depend heavily on YOUR perception of yourself and the thoughts that you nurture.

Words have the power to hurt and destroy but they also have the power to heal and create. If you keep speaking negative things *to* yourself and *about* yourself, more and more negative things are going to manifest for you.

Practice speaking POSITIVELY over your life. Look at yourself daily in the mirror and repeat affirmations. Cling to words of encouragement.

If you shift your mindset to one of hope, possibility and goodness, then negativity should not roll off your tongue. Speak little of your struggles and weaknesses. Your days may be hard and sometimes depressing, but as much as possible, refrain from talking about it constantly and especially to people who cannot provide solutions. Avoid people who speak more about hardships and woes than they do about goodness, solutions and ease.

We believe the things that we hear, over and over. If you are surrounded by people who speak negatively to you all of the time, at some point you are going to believe their words. One small insult that you hold on to becomes like a seed planted in your brain. In time, it will grow and poison the way you think about yourself.

None of us are 100% immune to criticism. As a gambler, you will receive a heap of negativity from family and friends when your habit depletes savings and creates debts. As much as people believe they have the right to vent, you also have the right to preserve your mental health. Their right to vocalize their pain is NOT greater than your right to heal.

You are allowed to grow and evolve.
If the people closest to you care about your recovery, then they should be willing to participate in it. If you have made the decision to live gamble-free and you are actively working towards wellness, then it is fair and within your rights to walk away from anyone who continuously puts you down. Let that person know who you are today. This version of yourself does not need a constant reminder of past mistakes.

Choose healthy speech.
Guard your ears.
Guard your tongue.

Focus on what you want more of.

STRENGTHEN YOUR NO!

Desire is never quenched.
You will experience a temporary moment of satisfaction when you get the thing you want but soon after, a desire will pop up for something else. This is human nature.

In recovery, there is a need for discipline and restraint. If you are serious about quitting, then you must strengthen your NO.

NO is like a muscle that needs to be worked regularly in order for it to be powerful. NO is a complete sentence. It doesn't require a follow up or justification. When family or friends suggest going to the casino or places where games are available, you owe it to your recovery to say NO.

Strengthen your NO by putting measures in place to prevent yourself from gambling.

Self-Exclusion is a method of quitting whereby you visit your favorite casino and ask to be banned. You will be given forms to fill out and you will supply them with a photograph of yourself / identification. The ban is legal and applies to all participating casinos within the self-exclusion coverage area.

If you've chosen to Self-Exclude and then find yourself at the casino, you can be arrested and charged for trespassing.

Self-Exclusion places the burden on other people to ensure that you do not gamble. In cases where security doesn't catch you at the door and you happen to slip inside, you will not be able to cash in any jackpots that you might win. The casino will still take any money that you have lost.

Self-Exclusion will not apply to regular businesses that have a few gaming machines on the side. It is only available at casinos that choose to participate in the Self-Exclusion program.

Gamban is a subscription software that blocks access to over 60,000 gambling websites and apps worldwide. It blocks everything that is transactional, including cryptocurrencies and trading websites. It can be installed on up to 15 of your devices. The cost of the service is minimal and you have the option to pay for it with debit and credit cards or through PayPal. You can pay monthly or yearly and there is a free 7-day trial. Gamban works well for persons who are addicted to online gambling.
Visit www.gamban.com for this service.

If there is someone in your life that you trust, you can appoint them to act as a Guardian for your money. This person will have sole access to your funds, while you relinquish control. They will hold your debit and credit cards and issue cash based on the budget you set.

Self-Exclusion, Gamban software and Financial Guardianship are secondary measures put in place for moments when your urge to gamble becomes unbearable. They are safety nets.

You hold the primary responsibility for your recovery. The onus is on you to avoid bars, restaurants and any other establishments where temptation lurks.

You have to police yourself.

ALL
MESSES
ARE
FIXABLE.

When negative emotions overwhelm you, just stop and breathe. Inhale and exhale deeply. Center yourself and remember that ALL messes are fixable. **No situation is so bad that you have to harm yourself.**

Make a choice to align your thoughts to positivity and also productivity. You do not need a New Year or even a new day to start. You can choose right now, in this moment, to cast off all negativity and to think better, healthier thoughts.

Naturally, there will be moments when you spiral downwards. You might remember all of your losses, debts and broken relationships. You might even be inclined to think and speak of yourself in a derogatory manner. When these moments pop up, just acknowledge them for what they are. These negative thoughts remind you of what has happened but they do not control the possibilities of your future.

The fact is, you WILL have money again. Through proper planning and financial management, your debts can be cleared. Your broken relationships can be mended and you can also create new bonds with new people.

Lean on the Gamblers Anonymous groups for support during difficult times. You might not feel comfortable airing your secrets to strangers but it's quite possible that they've heard it all before and won't judge you.

You might not agree with everything in their literature but you can **take what works and leave what doesn't.**

Your thoughts might be racing, you might even be irritable and lack the patience to listen. You might want to be the center of attention and get the answers you need quickly and it could be frustrating having to hear other people cry about their struggles. It takes empathy to listen to other people's stories and connect it with your own but empathy is something that a lot of gamblers lack. You are accustomed to being manipulative, secretive and untruthful, so being compassionate and supportive may prove to be a challenge.

The Gamblers Anonymous groups have been around for many years. Trust that they know what to expect from new members. Their program may not be everyone's cup of tea but it's a good place to start your Recovery journey.

It is wise to follow the advice of people who have first hand experience with what you're going through. The Gamblers Anonymous group members have been where you are and there is a strong commitment to recovery and an earnest dedication towards helping others.

This is where you can find a Sponsor and genuine support during difficult times. The program is free of charge and meetings are easily accessible. A quick search online can show you in-person and virtual meetings that are available at your convenience.

You are not destined to be a loser. You are not chained to failure. As long as you have breath in you, there are opportunities for change, growth and freedom.

Support is available.
Get out of your own way, reach out and accept the help.

WITHDRAWAL IS REAL.

Withdrawal is the dark hallway you have to walk through in order to reach the door of Recovery. If you turn back because it's difficult or scary, you will only prolong your healing.

Withdrawal symptoms could begin a few days after your last bet and continue for a few weeks. You are likely to experience many of the withdrawal symptoms that drug addicts do, including cold sweats, headaches, body shakes and nausea.

The 3rd, 4th and 5th day of withdrawal can be the most challenging. This is where you just have to go through the motions. Surrender to it. Cry. Vent. Pace. Shake. Sleep ...but remind yourself that it will pass. Because it will pass.

Surrender to what you are going through without consuming alcohol or sleeping pills. Eat the foods you love and drink lots of water.

Exercise if you get a burst of energy. Take a hot bath or visit a sauna for a good sweat. When the urge to gamble is strong, take a cold shower.

Reach out to a loved one for support and let them know that you are in crisis. Be open and honest with at least one person who is willing to participate in your Recovery.

Family members might not know the extent of your gambling disorder. They might not understand what gambling does to your brain, so they would not believe that withdrawal is real for you. Ask your loved one to read up on withdrawal, so that they know what to expect.

Keep reminding yourself that all of what you're feeling is normal. In a few days you will level out and be okay.

GET TO THE ROOT OF WHY YOU GAMBLE AND HEAL THAT.

As kids we can't wait to grow up and have our own house, buy fancy cars and make our own money. We yearn for independence from our parents and hope to find a soulmate who we can share the rest of our life with. These dreams die slow deaths when we branch out on our own and realize how heavy the weight of adulthood truly is.

We stay in miserable jobs just for the paycheck because a steady income keeps a roof over our head and food on the table. We never experience fairytale romances but instead end up with partners who cheat or nag us to death the minute we step into the house. Debt looms over us like a dark cloud and creditors pursue us like hound dogs. We look around and see other people living their best life and wonder why ours has to suck so much.

Most people look forward to the weekend where we can numb the pains of adulthood with some form of entertainment. While a lot of people enjoy the movies and restaurants, others go to the bars and clubs. Some escape their realities with drugs and alcohol while others find comfort in gambling.

The harder life gets, the more we want to run away from it.

When we don't have the answers or resources to make life better, we try to bury our head in something that could distract us and provide joy, even if it is short-lived. This is the way we cope.

"Escapism is mental diversion from unpleasant or boring aspects of daily life, typically through activities involving imagination or entertainment. Escapism may be used to occupy one's self away from persistent feelings of depression or general sadness." – Wikipedia.

GAMBLING TO ESCAPE BOREDOM

There is a void in your life. A feeling of emptiness ... and a frustration with this emptiness. You find it challenging to focus because you are unsatisfied and uninterested in the activities that you have to do on a regular basis. Your life feels uneventful and mundane.

The bright colors, flashing lights and up-tempo sounds of the games provide an escape and make you feel alive. They spark excitement into your dull day.

Keep record of the days, times, places and activities that you are doing when you experience boredom and feel the urge to gamble. These records will help you to identify triggers so that you can treat with your boredom in a proactive way.

Participate in activities that keep you mentally stimulated. You might find comfort in doing puzzles, crosswords, sudoku and mazes. If doing these provide no challenge for you, then create them. It could be that you are meant to be the Creator instead of the consumer. Create something interesting and put it up for sale.

Search yourself. What is your life's purpose? What are you most passionate about? What do you want your legacy to be? Set a goal for yourself and aim to complete it.

Go outside and connect with nature. Participate in physical activities that make you sweat and get your heart pumping. Learn to swim. Invest in some good shoes and take a run. Hit a ball. Go for a hike. Breathe fresh air.

Do more activities with your loved ones. If your family is busy or you do not have a good relationship with them, then connect with your friends. Join groups with people who are your own age and keep busy in activities that do not involve wagering money.

Create a bigger, bolder life. Make a conscious effort to experience new places, cultures and foods. Get off your devices and delve into the diversity of the world.

GAMBLING TO ESCAPE STRESS

Most of us deal with stress in a reactive way. We try to distance ourselves physically and psychologically from our problems and run towards activities that give us instant joy.

The games give an illusion of freedom. The minute you leave the casino or log off, reality jumps right back on your shoulders, with the added weight of wasted time and money.

Problems can only be fixed if they are dealt with head-on. If you are committed to improving your life then you must participate in activities that are healthy and solution-focused.

There is no shame in seeking professional support for problems that you are facing. The world is becoming more accepting of therapy and displays of vulnerability.

Meditation, yoga and journal writing are just some of the activities that people are encouraged to do, to become more mindful of their feelings and to balance themselves.

Make use of Positive Re-appraisal techniques whereby you look for the good in challenging situations. Focus on the things that you are grateful for and consciously work on developing an optimistic spirit.

Find the lessons in your trials. Turn your mess into a message. Strive to heal yourself so that you can turn around and help to free someone else.

The goal is to be proactive, to develop your coping skills and to embrace new ways of treating with your problems. Stay grounded in reality and avoid looking for a way to escape the things that are unpleasant or difficult.

GAMBLING AS PART OF YOUR IDENTITY

Do you feel connected to a particular game? Do you feel a connection so deep that you believe the game is part of who you are? Do you take pride in being someone who excels at that game and cannot seem to understand why other people would play games that are inferior to it?

Gamblers often form a connection with a particular game. You have your special seat that everyone knows is your spot. Other people rely on luck but you've played this game so many times that you've become a master of it. You operate with skill, not luck. You know the machine and can command it to do as you desire. You can will things into fruition. Losses are just slip ups. They are opportunities to regroup and get better.

These are the things the gambler believes.

Your gambling identity, your persona, only holds true within the walls of the casino. In the real world your actions are those of degenerates. You are seen as a loser who throws away your money and chooses a stupid game over your family.

Outside of the casino nobody cares that you had a royal flush. They don't care that the roulette ball landed in a different pocket then bounced out and hit your number. Regular people do not care about your lucky streaks.

Regular people want normal lives, with normal partners who care about normal things.

Being a high-roller might mean something in the gaming world but in reality has no value.

If you desire power and status then search out avenues where you can achieve them legitimately without having to wager money. Strive to achieve your accolades in a legitimate way. Live authentically.

GAMBLING TO FEEL LIKE A WINNER

Some people gamble in order to gain a sense of achievement. You need some form of confirmation that you are a success and that you can make things happen.

Life can be challenging. You might want certain things and not know exactly how to have them become a part of your reality.

The things that you want might be elusive and this causes you to feel like a loser. You gamble because games allow you the opportunity to win. It doesn't matter how big or small the jackpot, you participate simply for the feeling of being a winner.

Gambling trains your brain to prioritize instant gratification. You will prefer to indulge in activities that allow you to have instant achievement and instant gains. You will feel heavy and reluctant to strive for long term goals. The effect is that you will have pleasure in the moment but achieve nothing of substance in the long run.

Think about your life right now. What are the things you are most displeased with? What would you like to improve? What do you think is do-able within the next 90 days?

Create a plan for your life. Focus on things that you can do to improve your health, finances, relationships, spirituality, education and mental wellbeing. Set simple, realistic goals. Create a plan of action and commit to getting things done. Work on it every day and expect that you will have improvement in your circumstances, slowly but surely.

GAMBLING TO RECOUP LOSSES

Every single gambler has experienced this. Gambling in hopes of getting back what you've lost. You put more and more money into the game, not even aiming for a profit, but instead hoping just to recover what you've spent.

Think about how much money you've lost while gambling. Come up with an estimated figure and write it down. Now think about how much money you usually win and cash out on an average day. Write that figure down as well. How many days of successful gameplay and cashing out will it take for you to recover what you've lost?

Let's be real here. It is very difficult for you to cash out. No matter how much money you've won, you always think that you can do better and win more.

We've already established that gambling is entertainment. It is not a sustainable way to generate income. Make peace with your losses because the money is gone. You will never win it all back with profit. NEVER! Stop digging that hole before it becomes a financial grave. Accept that you've lost. **Accept the fact that true wealth, long-lasting wealth, does not come from playing games.**

GAMBLING BECAUSE YOU LOVE THE GAME

Gambling makes you happy. You love the game and feel a special joy when playing. If it weren't for the financial losses and devastating consequences, you could see yourself playing all the time.

Gambling is like being in an abusive relationship. You know it hurts. Everyone sees your pain and advises you to leave. You know there's no healthy future together but it's difficult to walk away. You're focused on the good in your partner and hope that they will change but they keep mistreating you and then reeling you back in when you try to quit.
The connection is toxic.

Science has proven that gambling affects your brain. When you're winning and even when you're losing, your brain produces dopamine, endorphins and adrenaline. These help you to feel pleasure. They trigger positive feelings in your body and increase excitement no matter the outcome of your game.

The games themselves are designed to be short so that you won't become bored easily. This creates a situation where every minute or so your brain floods itself with hormones that make you feel happy.

The longer you play, the more your brain gets accustomed to this instant rush of happiness. In the end, activities that take long to release “happy-hormones” will no longer be of interest to you.

You are entitled to love whatever you love. However, you are only misleading yourself when you think that the game owes you a financial reward in return for your devotion. The fact is, when you gamble, you are purchasing very expensive entertainment. The game is designed to profit its Owner and to strip the consumer of money, time and patience.

How long are you going to love this thing that is designed to hurt you? How long will you choose to stay in this abusive relationship?

Gambling promotes a sedentary, empty lifestyle. You sit indoors, facing a screen for hours and hours. Consider taking up an outdoor sport to get your heart pumping and to receive an adrenaline rush. There are many affordable, and also free, forms of entertainment that you can engage in by yourself or with your loved ones.

Participating in activities with your family not only brings enjoyment to the group but it helps to strengthen bonds and repair broken relationships. Everyone benefits in a wholesome manner.

GAMBLING FOR FRIENDSHIP

While friendships are easy for some people to form, others struggle to belong. It seems like everyone already has their tribe and it is difficult to be let in. While casinos provide a rich playground for socialization, Recovery requires you to choose environments that are wholesome, to develop the interpersonal relationships that you crave.

You are never too odd or old to make new friends. Someone, somewhere, will like you and accept you as you are. Decide that you are going to be brave and put yourself out there.

Search for groups online and in your community and strive to participate in a new activity. Look within the Gamblers Anonymous groups. It is not a guarantee that you will find a forever friend but who knows, you just might.

GAMBLING BECAUSE OF A SELF-DEFEATING PERSONALITY DISORDER

We've discussed several root causes of gambling but this one, the Self-Defeating Personality Disorder is one that you should ideally explore in detail with a licensed therapist.

This disorder causes the person who experiences it to continuously engage in activities that are counter-productive. You gamble as a form of self-sabotage, repeatedly choosing to bet when you know that it will lead to disappointment, failure and mistreatment. Subconsciously, you want to lose everything because you want to punish yourself.

Rock bottom is actually your comfort zone.

You are accustomed to living in a deprived state, stretching a dollar and neglecting yourself. You have a poor sense of self worth. When you lose your money and people say hurtful things to you, it only confirms the bad things that you already say to yourself. You gamble to incite anger and rejection from people in order to feel hurt and humiliated. You are accustomed to pain and struggle, and thrive off it.

You enjoy having a secret life and find freedom in

being a deviant. You are exhausted with societal rules and the obligation to be on your best behavior. Gambling allows you to remove your halo and explore your dark side without caution.

You are agitated when life is smooth, so you gamble to create chaos. You need the extreme highs and lows to avoid the monotony of life. As your tolerance to risk increases, you have to seek bigger thrills. You gamble money but are subconsciously wagering relationships, friendships and jobs.

Losses have a way of making you feel brave and even resilient. While the average person would bow out of a game after losing a mere $20, you can experience losses in the thousands and not even flinch. You almost brag about your biggest losses because it amazes people that you had that large quantity of money to begin with and that you could sustain such a hit without falling apart.

The Self-Defeating Personality Disorder was last mentioned in the Diagnostic and Statistical Manual of Mental Disorders, Third Edition (DSM-3). It was not included in the DSM-4 or DSM-5 because of its overlap with the Borderline, Avoidant and Dependent Personality Disorders.

Because of the severity of this disorder, it is best to seek professional treatment from a licensed psychiatrist who can devise a plan of action and treatment that is specific to your needs.

GAMBLING FOR THE MONEY

You gambled, got lucky and realized that it is an easy way to multiply your funds. You continue to play in hopes of securing another big win.

You rebrand your gambling as a side hustle and business and consider your initial wager to be capital that you are investing. You set a daily quota and play until that amount is made or until your capital runs out.

On this journey of recovery it is important to identify your money mindset. Search yourself. How do you feel about money? Do you feel a scarcity? Are you afraid that you do not have enough to survive?

Do you prefer to get money fast, even if it is by less than wholesome means? Do you desire to have a big amount of money so that you can do something grand?

Casinos and online games turn your money into tokens and credits so that it doesn't feel like real money. It's now a chip or a shiny gold coin ... not eight hours worth of labor. **They want you to feel disconnected from the struggle of earning your money so that you will freely play it away.** Only when you lose it all do you remember that it's real money and remember all of the important things that it could have paid for.

How many times have you refused to purchase something at a store because it was expensive, yet wasted thousands in gaming without reservation?

If any of this sounds familiar, then you know that you have a warped money mindset that needs to be adjusted.

The fast and easy road does not guarantee a reward. **You often spend thousands, to win crumbs.** You never win enough money that could change your life for good but you wager enough money to risk losing your family and quality of life.

Consider how much money you earn per hour. When the urge to gamble pops up, think of how many hours of labor it is really costing you. Do the math.

Losing $X,XXX costs me XX hours of labor.
You will see that you are literally paying and playing with your life.

LEAVE
THE
GAMES
FOR
THE
KIDS.

Finance occupies a prominent role at the core of your life. You get up each day and work because you need money. It's a bonus when you love your job and it gives you purpose, but money is the main reason why you labor.

Your primary daily focus is to obtain money because the amount you have, determines the quality of life you get to live. To have little money brings scorn and dis-ease while wealth brings adoration, power and freedom.

Money itself is neither good nor evil. It is merely a tool used to facilitate the exchange of goods and services from one person to another. Money allows us to live comfortably and enables access to experiences that fuel our joy and broadens our perspective.

Gamblers seldom think of money as a tool.
You like the *idea* of having more money but you do not crave the higher lifestyle that more money can bring. You are not focused on enjoying the money. All you really want is the win.

What important things have you done with the cash you've won? Were you able to purchase a home or car? Did you sponsor a family vacation? Did you use your jackpot to purchase a new wardrobe or treat yourself to a day at the spa? Do you actually use your winnings to improve the quality of your life? Are you ever able to cash out and be satisfied or does it all go back into the game?

You spend the majority of your life in pursuit of money, yet do not set aside time to manage it properly. This poor money management leads to financial bondage.

BUDGETING

This is a financial management practice that allows you to see how much money you have and where it is being spent. It also allows you to reduce expenditure, facilitates the purchase of assets and positions you to be financially prepared for emergencies.

The hardest part of budgeting is the discipline to stick to it. You can crunch the numbers all day but without the effort to be loyal to that budget you will not have growth.

If you repeatedly tell yourself that you're bad at managing your money then you'll train your brain to accept being bad with money. At some point you have to do some serious adulting and take the necessary steps to create the reality you want. It starts by generating a financial plan and sticking to it no matter what.

Set aside a day and time each week for money management. It's best to have a weekly review so that the habit is formed properly and the goals stay fresh in your mind. You can also avoid the build-up and heaviness of sorting through bills and receipts if you break them up and deal with them in small portions weekly.

Choose a time when your home is calm and quiet. Let your family members know that you will be taking an hour or two of personal time and you do not want to be unnecessarily disturbed.

Get in the habit of requesting and keeping your receipts, even if it's just for small purchases. When sorting through all of those receipts you will be surprised at how easily your money escapes you on the purchase of frivolous items.

Make a list of all your sources of income and then list your expenses so that you have an idea of the numbers you're working with. You will have expenses like clothing and eating at restaurants that you may not have an exact monthly figure for. In those instances just list the expense and give an average of how much you might spend.

If your salary is automatically deposited into your bank account each month it would be beneficial to create a separate account for the purpose of saving. Having all of your money pooled into one account will not allow you to properly see your growth and could actually encourage unnecessary spending.

Put your money into different banks.
You can deposit millions of dollars into your bank account but only a certain amount of it will be insured. If the bank goes out of business, they are only liable to repay you up to a maximum amount of $250,000 in the United States and $85,000 in the UK.

This is the maximum payout per customer, per bank. Even if your money is split amongst several accounts, you will only be compensated up to that amount in total.

CALENDARING

Treat your people well. Get a calendar and highlight the birthdays of your children and spouse. Take note of anniversaries, graduations and holidays. Whatever dates are important, write it down and decide in advance how you are going to celebrate. Buy gifts at least 1-month in advance and hide them away.

Your family should not have to bear the weight of your gambling or have to suffer because of your vices. They should not be forced to sink on your ship.

Your children deserve to have cake on their birthday and toys at Christmas. They deserve to have parties and extracurricular activities and it is your responsibility as a parent to have the money to make these things possible.

SAVING

Priority has to be given to the retention of earnings. Too often we do not actively focus on saving. Money sits in the bank and we consider it savings until a need arises and then we dip into it.

If you really want to grow your money, make a withdrawal before you spend a cent from your paycheck and deposit it into an untouched savings account. Pay yourself before you pay any bill. One day you will be too old to work and will need this money to survive.

Wealth is not about how much money you make, but rather how much of it you keep. Save with purpose. Be deliberate about it. Know exactly what you are saving for and commit to it. Do not focus on the dollar amount and think that your contributions are too small to matter. Your focus here is on working your saving muscle and developing the habit of living proactively. Focus on the percentage that you are saving and trust that it will add up. Little by little you can grow something for yourself.

INVESTING

What do you think would happen if you buried a $100 bill and watered it every day? A child who doesn't know any better might expect a money tree to sprout but a right-thinking adult will know that this cannot happen.

Your money will rot in the ground and you will be left with regret when you consider all the productive things you could have done with that money if you made a better decision. This is what happens when you invest in schemes that promise to get you rich quickly.

Forex and cryptocurrency markets are volatile and carry substantial risks but they seem attractive to people who believe that they are an appropriate way to get rich fast. These people seldom think of themselves as gambling, but essentially that's what it is.

Avoid investing in things that you do not understand or things that cannot be explained simply. Avoid what seems too good to be true and what is said to be available only to a select few. Remember that the only free cheese is the one sitting in the trap. You will be punished for your greed by losing your investment while the person who swindled you out of your money profits off your gullibility.

Smart investing starts with knowledge. Seek information and advice from qualified individuals who have a proven track record of success.

Consult professionals who understand the state of the economy at present and are passionate about current and relevant strategies for generating profits.

PAY WHAT YOU OWE.

DEBT REPAYMENT

Stop borrowing money. You will never be free to experience a life of ease if you keep shackling yourself to loans.

Make a list of all the people you owe and the outstanding amounts owed to them. Pay the people closest to you first. If you've borrowed money from family and friends, settle those debts before you tackle anything else. Clearing those debts is a simple way to start mending broken relationships. As you journey to heal your life, it would be helpful to have the support of these people. Don't let money be the reason why family and friends sever ties with you.

Credit card debt is the worst form of financial bondage that you can experience. A cycle is created where you are obligated to only pay the minimum amount due and then it becomes available again for you to spend.

Credit cards are useful in situations where you have no available funds but every time you swipe your card, you are chaining yourself to a system that is designed to exploit you.

The system is set up whereby a good credit history is needed to secure a mortgage or rent a space to live. Business owners are even performing credit checks before they commit to hiring, so you cannot adopt an all or nothing approach. You may not be able to control the system as a whole but you can control your spending. The onus is you to purchase wisely and repay responsibly, to ensure that the credit system works to your benefit.

As soon as you set aside your savings, withdraw money for the repayment of debts. Pay off the credit card with the highest interest rate first and then proceed with the others. Make your payments on time. If you absolutely must use your credit card, swipe sensibly. Don't destroy your credit on junk. Limit yourself to one credit card and be mindful of the interest rates and annual fees.

Put your tax refund towards the repayment of your debts. As much as possible, stick to cash transactions and do not enter into hire purchase contracts where you are liable to pay exorbitant interest fees. Save so that you can purchase the things you want without using credit. Delay your indulgences and know that it will benefit you in the long run.

EXPENSE REDUCTION

No financial plan is complete without fat trimming. Although it is not necessary to become a cheapskate, a diligent effort must be made to reduce your expenses.

Bills are the heart and soul of your budget and the place where you need to crunch numbers the most. Essential bills are the mortgage or rent, insurance, food, utilities and car payments. Your primary focus is to reduce these costs and to keep them from absorbing more than 40% percent of your income.

Telephone and data plans, WiFi, extra-curricular activities, gym memberships and hobbies are expenses that can be reduced. You can eliminate one bill by abandoning the house phone since everyone carries a cellphone nowadays. Streaming services offer a variety of programming and are a cheaper alternative to cable and satellite TV.

The internet that you are already paying for offers many free weightloss meal plans and workouts, so the gym membership can also be ditched. You can purchase quality fitness equipment and create your own workout space at home, which will save you time and money.

Source recipes online and try to prepare meals with your family instead of dining out. Imagine for a second how happy your family will be to see you evolve from a person who spends all your free time gambling, to one who is proud to be a present spouse and parent. Home cooked meals are less expensive than dining out, they are healthier and preparing them with your family helps to strengthen emotional bonds.

Take a detailed assessment of your lifestyle and pinpoint the things that you do not really need or use on a regular basis. Try to cut from this in such a way that your family still has access to their favorite pastimes, without feeling deprived.

TAKE THE LEAD.

The key to financial abundance is Ownership. Own a business. Create a product for sale or offer a service whereby you can generate income. **Be more of a Creator and less of a Consumer.**

As an employee you sell your labor, your time and essentially your life for a price that someone else says you're worth. You dedicate forty years of your skills and creativity to building someone else's wealth and legacy. You follow their rules and plans in exchange for the assumed security of a paycheck.

The employer may be less qualified than you, yet he enjoys a higher quality of life because he secured some capital and started a business. As an employee, you build your entire life on the success of your employer's dreams. Do not expect security or fairness. When business is bad, he will cut staff before cutting into his own profits. If his business fails, you will be on the breadline.

No matter how saturated the market may appear to be, new companies are always going to be built. You have the option of being a Leader or a Laborer. You can either build your own or spend your life building someone else's.

We often see the genius in other people but not ourselves. We praise their potential but discredit our own by holding on to the false belief that we aren't good enough and that we don't have what it takes to be the leader.

Life could be so much bigger, richer and fulfilling if we gave ourselves permission to try instead of shutting down our ideas. Every company that you see and patronize was once the dream of someone who dared to make it a reality. That person didn't have all the answers at first but they silenced their inner critic enough to give their dream a chance to grow.

We tend to think of businesses as faceless corporations but somebody sits at the helm. Somebody dreamed big, then woke up one day and started a bank. Somebody felt passionate about their recipes and started a restaurant, while someone else felt that they were stylish enough to start a clothing brand. They assessed what they could accomplish on their own and then partnered with others to make it a reality.

You have the money to get started. The thousands that you sink into gambling could be used to purchase assets and infrastructure that can produce a product or facilitate the delivery of a service. You also have the time that's required to grow a business. The hours and hours that you dedicate to the game can be put towards the growth of a legitimate business venture.

As a gambler, you are consuming entertainment. You will never generate enough winnings to change your life in a drastically positive way. Strive to be a Creator. Strive for Ownership. Buy tangible assets. Build a business that you can pass down to your children so that they never have to beg for opportunities at a stranger's table. Search your talents. Pick one idea. Create a plan of action, then stand prominently at the front and lead the persons who you hire to build your legacy.

Money that you generate from consistent labor is called Active Income. Your constant physical presence and effort are necessary if you want to earn it. If you cease action, you will not be paid. From a very young age we are urged to study hard so that we can get a job that pays a good salary ... an Active income.

Passive Income is generated from a business that requires minimal participation from you once it is set up. For example, if you write a book it only needs to be done one time however, the book can sell and generate a passive income for many years.

Wealthy persons have several streams of income, whereas the average individual has one or two jobs that usually generate active incomes. If you only focus on active income streams, your earning potential will be capped and you can be left physically burnt out. In such situations, when you cannot physically work, your finances will become paralyzed.

You cannot become rich from cutting expenses. You become financially free by creating multiple streams of income.

Schedule time to create a business plan. What are the resources available to you? What are the needs of those closest to you? What services are needed in your community? Begin with something simple that has a low startup cost. Resist the urge to take out a loan to start your business. If you have limited resources, it is best to operate where the risk is lowest by starting a service-based business.

Stop canceling your ideas and telling yourself that you are not capable of bringing them to fruition. You aren't a loser if you fail to accomplish something on your first try, or even on your twentieth. You only lose when you make the decision to quit for good because you believe that you don't have what it takes to succeed.

While some people get through Life in a seemingly easy way, others have to put in extra effort and flop multiple times before they see results. This is perfectly normal and okay. There is always time to learn and grow your competence. **The only limits that exist are the ones you place on yourself.**

Recovery is not merely about quitting gambling. It is about the holistic treatment and expansion of the mind. Recovery is about transformation and evolution, and education has a major role in this process.

If you are serious about turning your life around and becoming more of a Creator, it would be worthwhile to focus on learning new things.

FORGIVE AND BE FREE!

Forgiveness is a conscious decision to heal.
It is an awareness that the past cannot be changed and an acceptance of that fact. When you forgive, you make a decision to move forward without the weight of bitterness and regret. Forgiveness is not a pardon or a condoning of evil. It is simply a choice to heal from the hurt, for your own benefit.

Forgiving yourself is one of the hardest things to do, especially if you believe that you aren't worthy of forgiveness. It seems almost boldface to forgive yourself when you keep repeating the same mistakes, creating debts, lying to your loved ones and wasting so much time gambling but Forgiveness of Self is necessary. Nothing will change if you hold on to the shame and regret, and continue to punish yourself for your mistakes.

You are going to face challenges in life and because you are an imperfect human being, you are going to make mistakes along the way. Extend some grace to yourself. Be kind to yourself. Make a commitment to become a better version of yourself. Embrace what is positive and fulfilling, and allow yourself to be free.

HEAL.

EVOLVE.

MAKE APPROPRIATE CHOICES

If you donate $20,000 towards the building of a church or give it to charity, you will be praised for your generosity. If you lose $20,000 through gambling, your family will be upset. In both scenarios you will have $20,000 less in your bank account but people will respect you differently based on what you did with the money. In this example it's a case of morality. Charity is viewed as good, while gambling has a negative stigma attached to it.

If you won $20,000 you will be celebrated and possibly envied because people love and embrace winners. They despise losses because it affects their livelihood and they despise the risk you take with their quality of life. Nobody enjoys debt and lack. People want to have nice things. They crave stability and security, and money is the tool which facilitates this.

When you gamble, you wager your loved one's happiness and trust. When you gamble and lose, all they see is you making their lives harder, over a game. People do not want to be attached to someone who could potentially cause them to lose everything.

Spouses want to be loved and they want to be treated as a priority. They want you to make time for the relationship and to enjoy being with them. Nobody wants to compete with a casino or gambling website for attention.

If you want to maintain good relationships with family, friends and co-workers then you have to act in ways that are socially appropriate. You have to make choices that bring happiness and growth to the group. Gambling often brings devastation and embarrassment. It will never be an appropriate choice.

Own your mistakes. Learn your lessons and heal. Speak about your experiences without fear or shame. Declare your truth and cleanse your spirit.

Put in the work to build back a good reputation. Consciously combat the negativity that your gambling has caused. Turn your mess into a message of hope so that you can help someone else through their recovery.

Seize control of the narrative and do not allow anyone to use your past against you.

Engage in random acts of goodness.
Volunteer your time at a shelter, soup kitchen or other charitable organization. Plant a community garden or help to restore a communal space. Raise awareness about a problem and work towards a solution. Aim to be known as a person who does things for the improvement of your community.

Do as much good as you can to counteract the negativity of your gambling past. Let your light shine so bright that it overpowers the dark spirit of anyone who tries to bring you down to their level.

HEAL BROKEN RELATIONSHIPS

Getting out of debt is significantly easier than rebuilding broken trust. You can read several books on improving your financial life but there is no step by step manual that is proven to mend broken hearts.

At this point, nobody cares what you have to say. They've heard all of the empty promises before, so your words will be met with skepticism and scorn. **Your loved ones want to see consistent, improved behavior.** They don't want to hear you talk about quitting. They want to see you put in the work.

They want to see you self exclude, appoint a financial guardian, get a sponsor, participate in meetings, journal, rebuild your reputation, create and stick to a budget, repay your debts and heal. They want to see growth.

Create time for your partner and focus on the little things that you can do to make them feel loved. Gestures like buying jewelry or going to expensive restaurants might come across as manipulative and insincere. Your partner wants consistency. They want you to be thoughtful and to do things without being asked.

If you have intentions of returning to the game, spare your loved ones the heartbreak and do not make them any promises. Do not waste their time saying sorry and then revert back to your old ways.

Make amends when you've truly come to the end of your gambling journey and are genuinely remorseful for the pain you've caused. Do not apologize because it's on the list of things to do in your 12 step program.

Apologize because it is the right thing to do, not because you are searching for forgiveness. **Do not apologize with the expectation of a pardon.** People have the right to feel how they feel. They are allowed to shut you out and not respond to you in a positive manner. You are the offender and you are not in control of their healing. You have to respect their boundaries.

A person has to be open to having a conversation with you and open to receiving an apology. If your friends and family are not interested in hearing what you have to say, then you just have to be okay with that. They owe you nothing.

Put in the work and heal for your own benefit. Trust is slowly rebuilt when your loved ones see your consistent determination to be healthy and to do right. It could take years to be fully trusted again but it is possible.

Gamblers need money to play.
You need your job in order to generate these funds. You need to have proper hygiene and maintain a certain standard of appearance in order to gain entry into the casino. You need electricity, internet connections and electronic devices in order to gamble online. A person simply cannot whittle down to vagrancy and still expect to gamble.

But gambling takes away your money, homes, jobs and families in the long run. No matter how much you try to manage our gambling, the game takes significantly more than it rewards.

How then can you continue to choose this thing which only leads to your destruction?

Your feet will walk the path that your mind first envisions. If gambling is always in your thoughts, then your body will eventually end up at the casino or gambling websites.

What is the vision that you have for your life? What are your dreams, goals and desires? What is it that you hope to accomplish? Your vision matters. Spend some time thinking about your way forward. Who is the person that you hope to be a year from now?

When you truly want a gambling-free life, you'll do the work to secure your freedom. Nobody can rush your growth or force you to want better for yourself. That desire for a more meaningful life has to come from within and you have to consciously transform into the kind of person you want to be.

Recovery is not punishment. It is not boring or unfulfilling. Recovery actually brings peace and ease. It means having money, growing money in a legitimate way, having healthy relationships and building a good reputation.

***

Counting gamble-free days gives too much importance to something that is already dead. I believe in burying everything that has to do with gambling and just moving forward. Counting gamble-free days keeps gambling fresh and present in the mind. It keeps the mind focused on the past instead of on things that bring freedom and growth.

People get so caught up in counting days that it becomes their whole personality. It's like chaining yourself to a rotting carcass and dragging it with you for the rest of your life. How can this be freedom?

Too often we buy into traditional ways of doing things. We believe that it is the right and proper way but never consider if it's actually working for our benefit.

Counting gamble-free days might have value to some people but it could be detrimental to the mental wellbeing of others. When a person relapses, they have the added weight of disappointment for not making it past a certain number of days. They're back to the shame of Day 1 while other people brag about making their 90+ days. It brings an element of failure and unworthiness into something that should just be about living a healthy, balanced life.

If counting gamble-free days works for you then do it but if the practice makes you feel like a failure, then let it go. Your recovery doesn't have to look like anybody else's to be valid.

You are not weak or powerless. You made certain choices and those choices have consequences. Make better decisions and fix your life.

The Devil didn't make you gamble and God isn't responsible for patching things up. You need to stop wallowing in self-pity and start doing some serious adulting.

Stop looking for someone else to do the work that you are supposed to do. Look in the mirror and hold that person accountable.

No amount of prayer is going to reduce your debt. Get off your knees and create a financial plan. Put preventative measures in place and find a way to grow your money legitimately.

Remember that gambling is a business that benefits its Owner. It will NEVER give you all of the riches you desire.

The choice to quit gambling is ultimately yours. Invest in your own life or keep making the billionaire Owners wealthier. **You have the power to choose the juicy steak or to settle for the crumbs.**

www.ingramcontent.com/pod-product-compliance
Ingram Content Group UK Ltd.
Pitfield, Milton Keynes, MK11 3LW, UK
UKHW021924190726
13853UKWH00002B/824

9 798215 918104